Blossom

A Grayscale Coloring Book

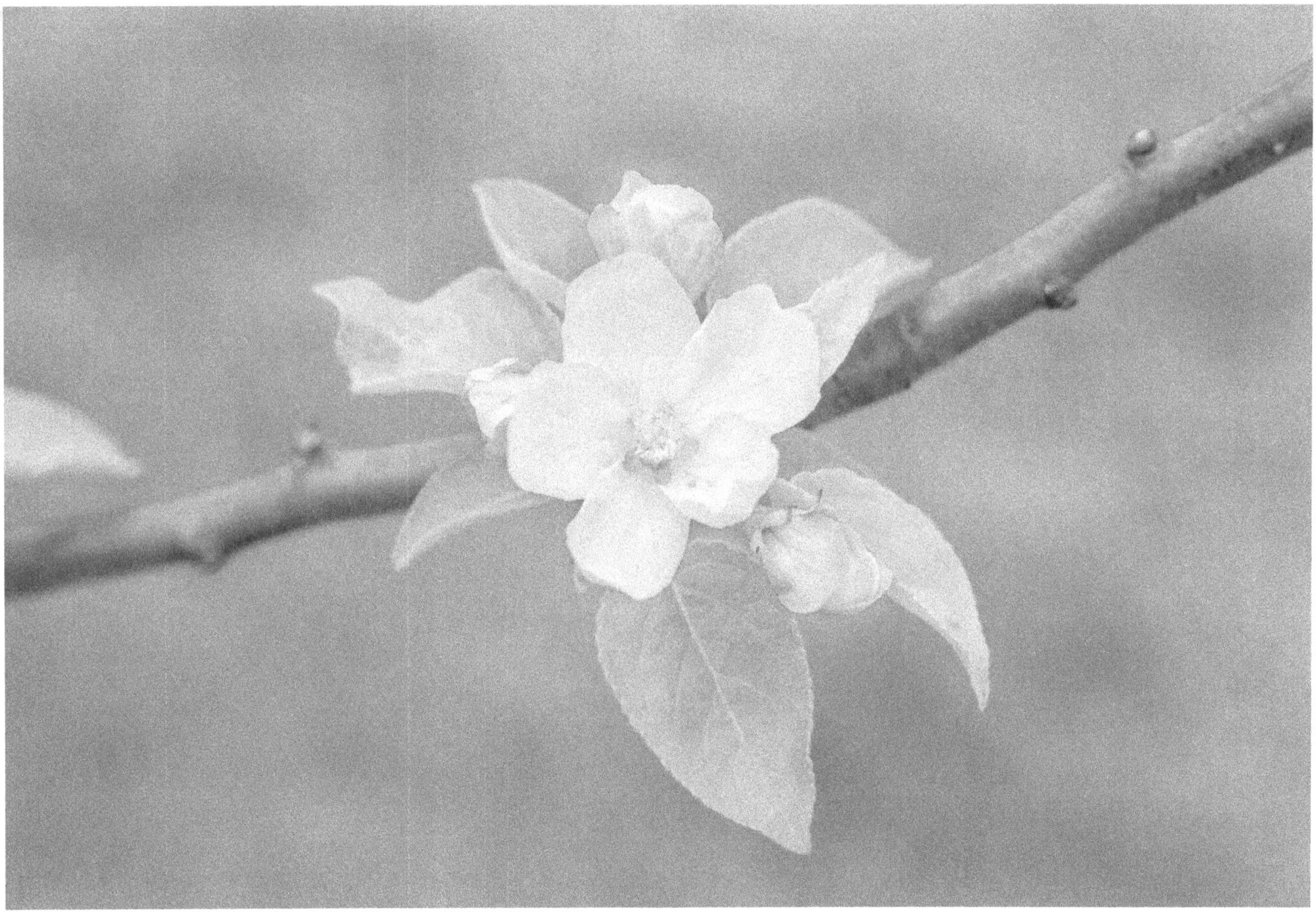

Madeline Rose

Blossom is a collection of photographs taken by me, a college student and photographer, for my third Grayscale coloring book. It is a photographic collection of beautiful flowers and landscapes taken during springtime in New England. I hope you enjoy coloring these pages as much as I enjoyed taking the pictures!

Madeline

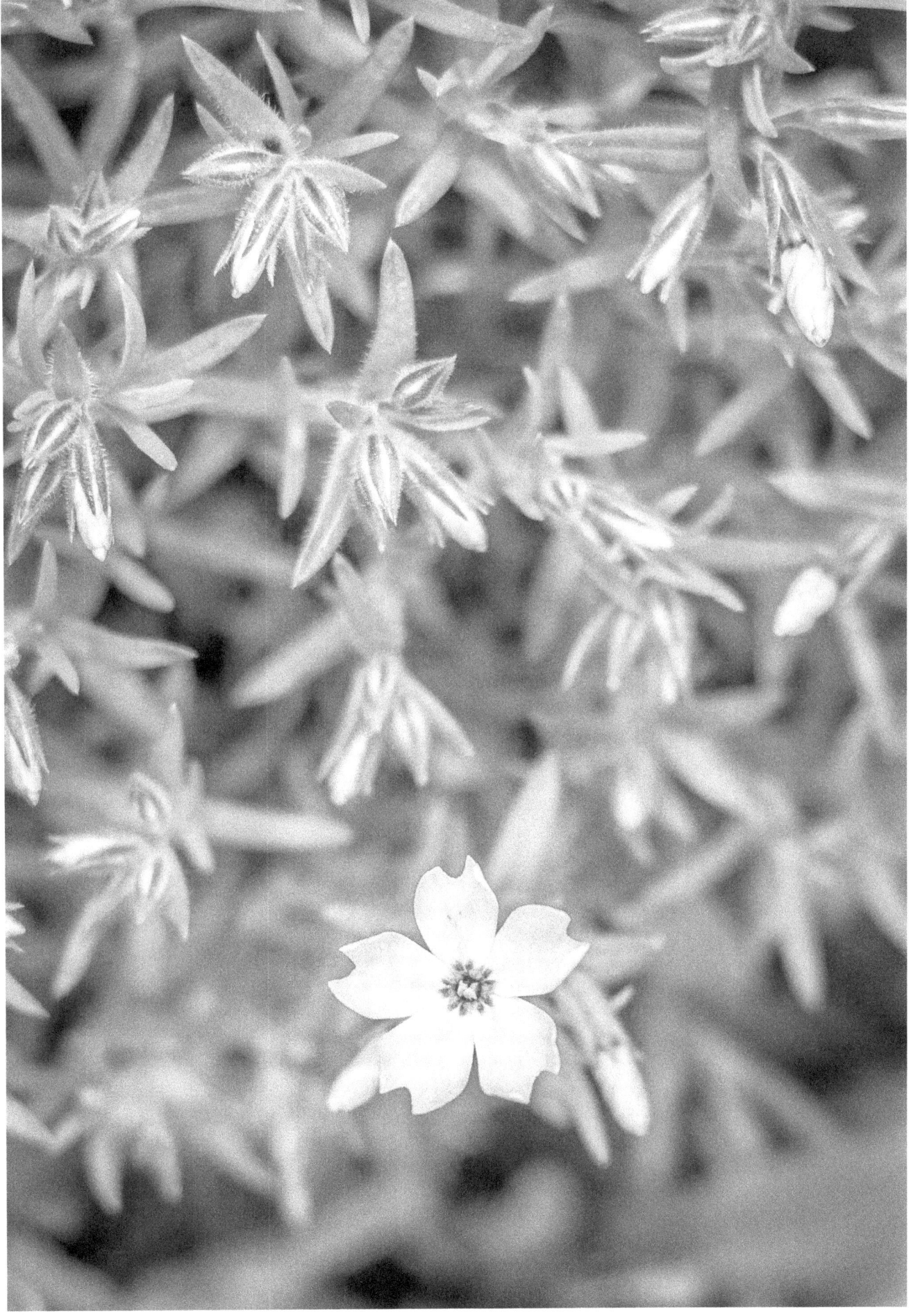

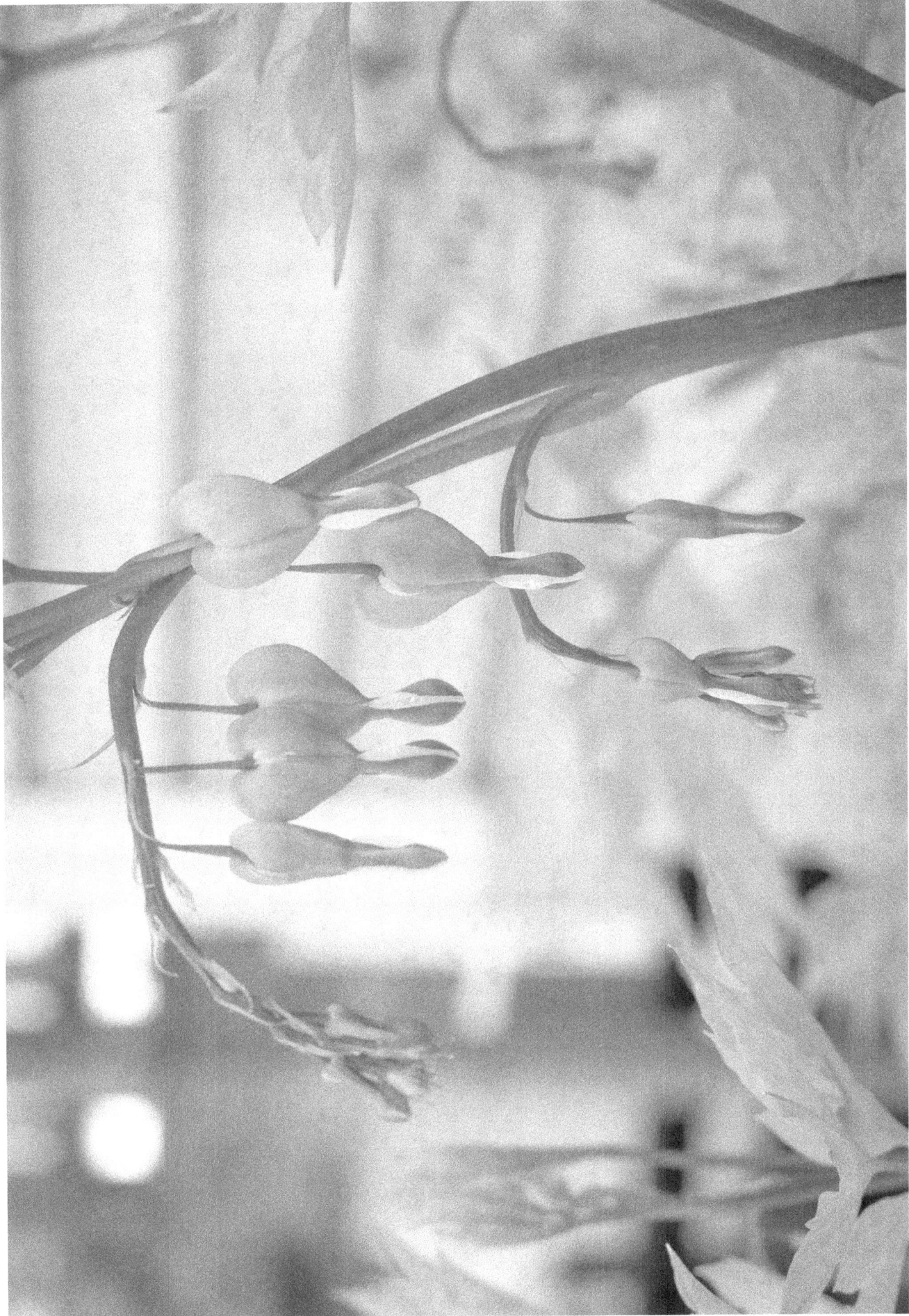

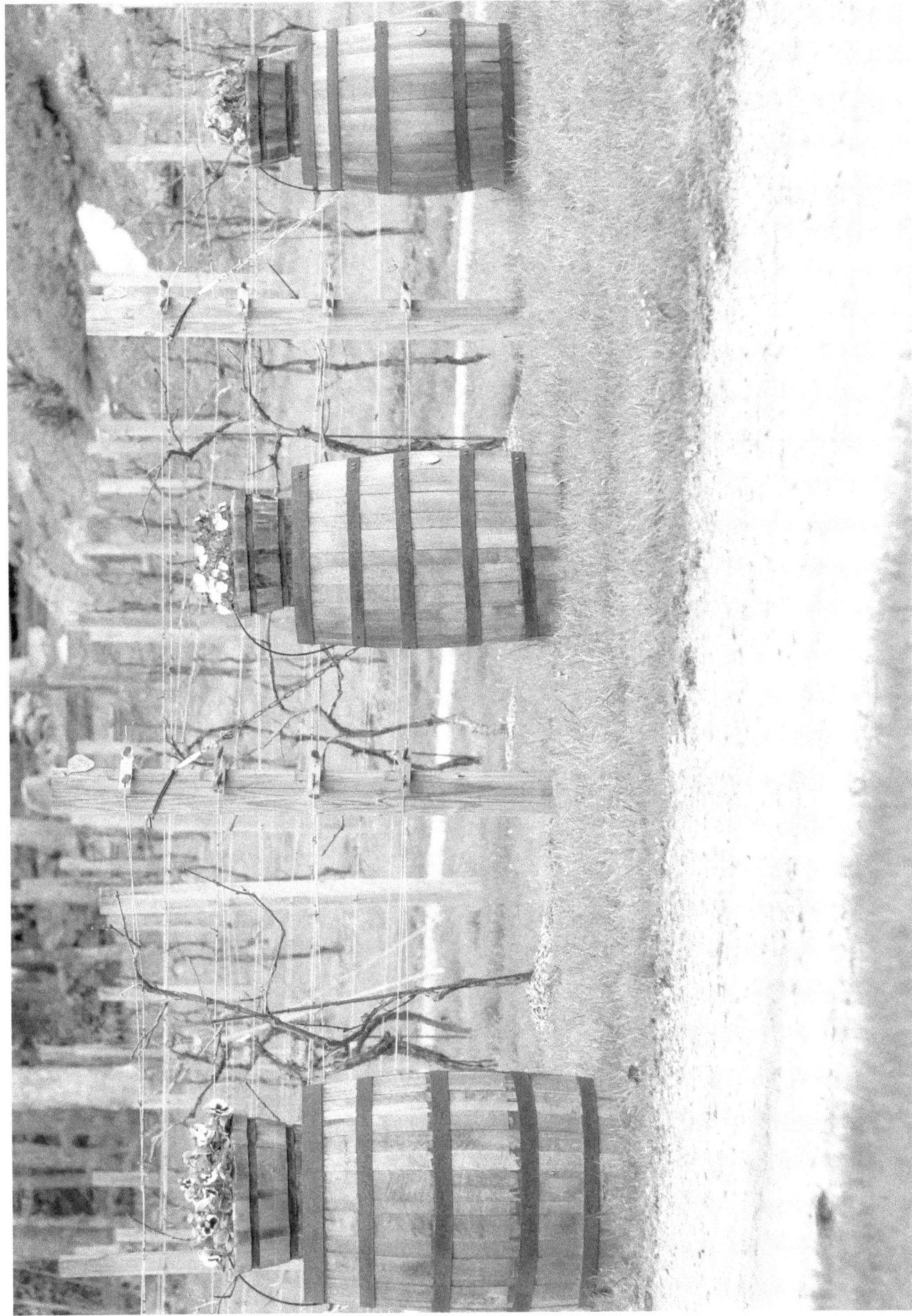

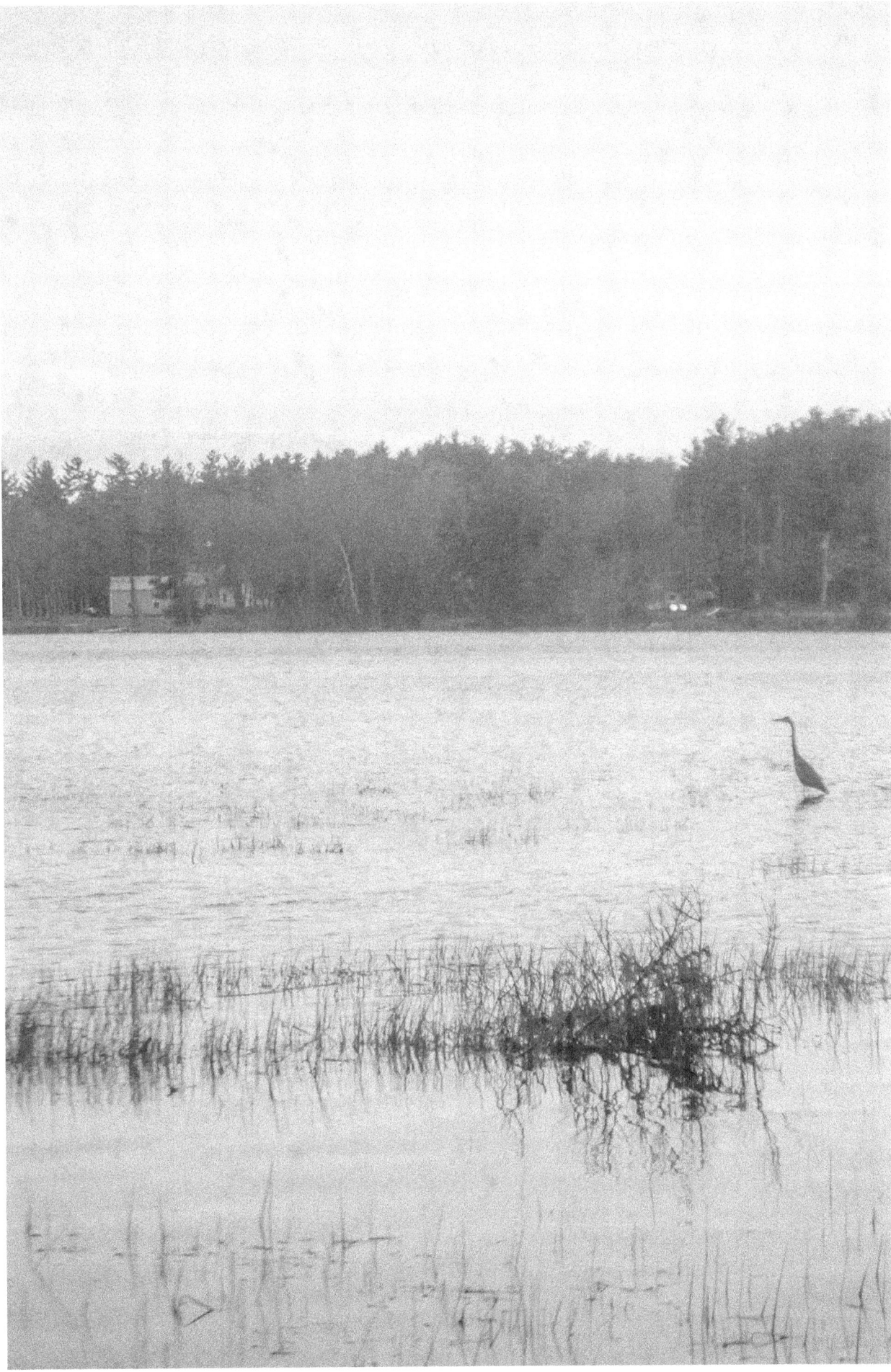

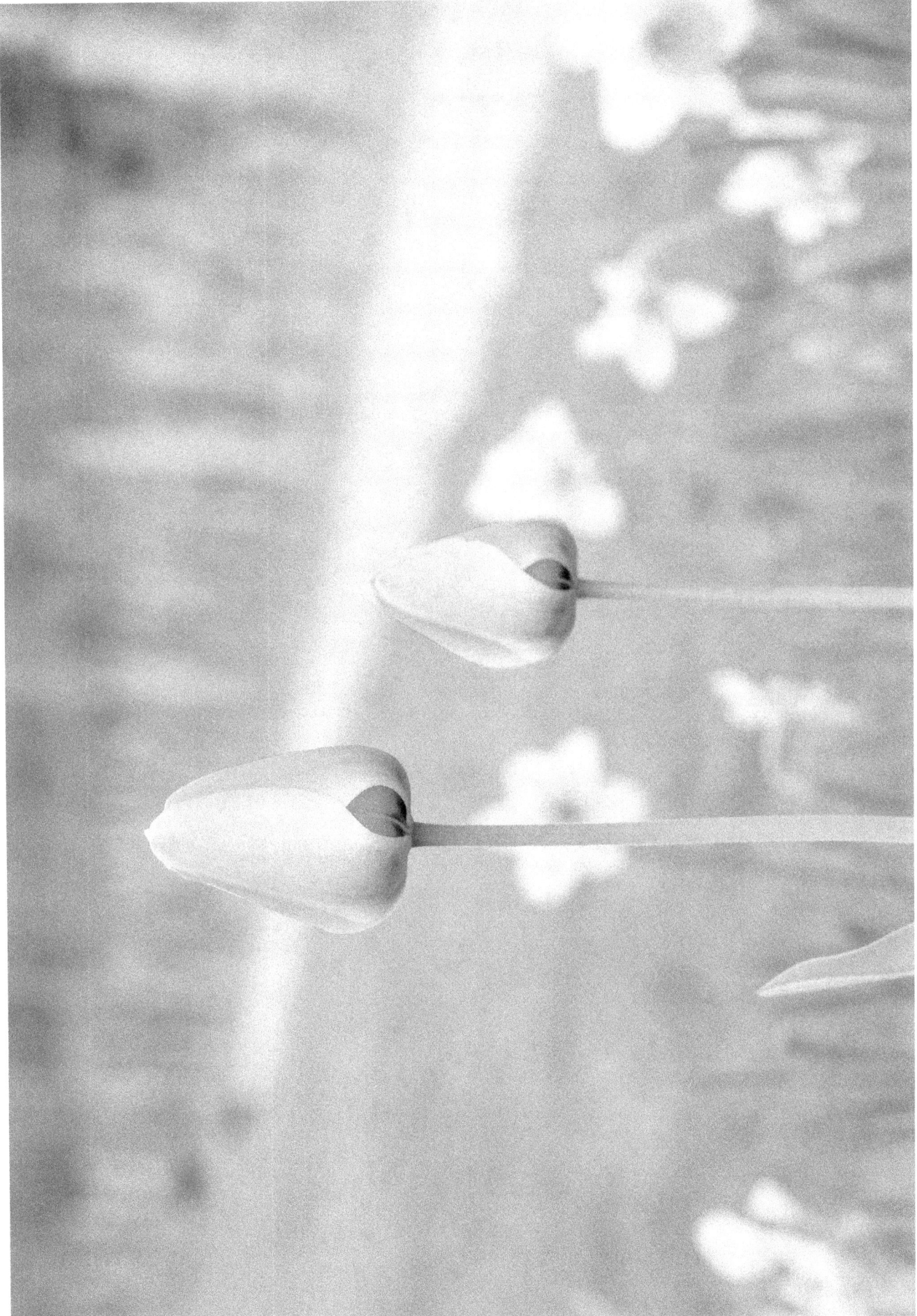

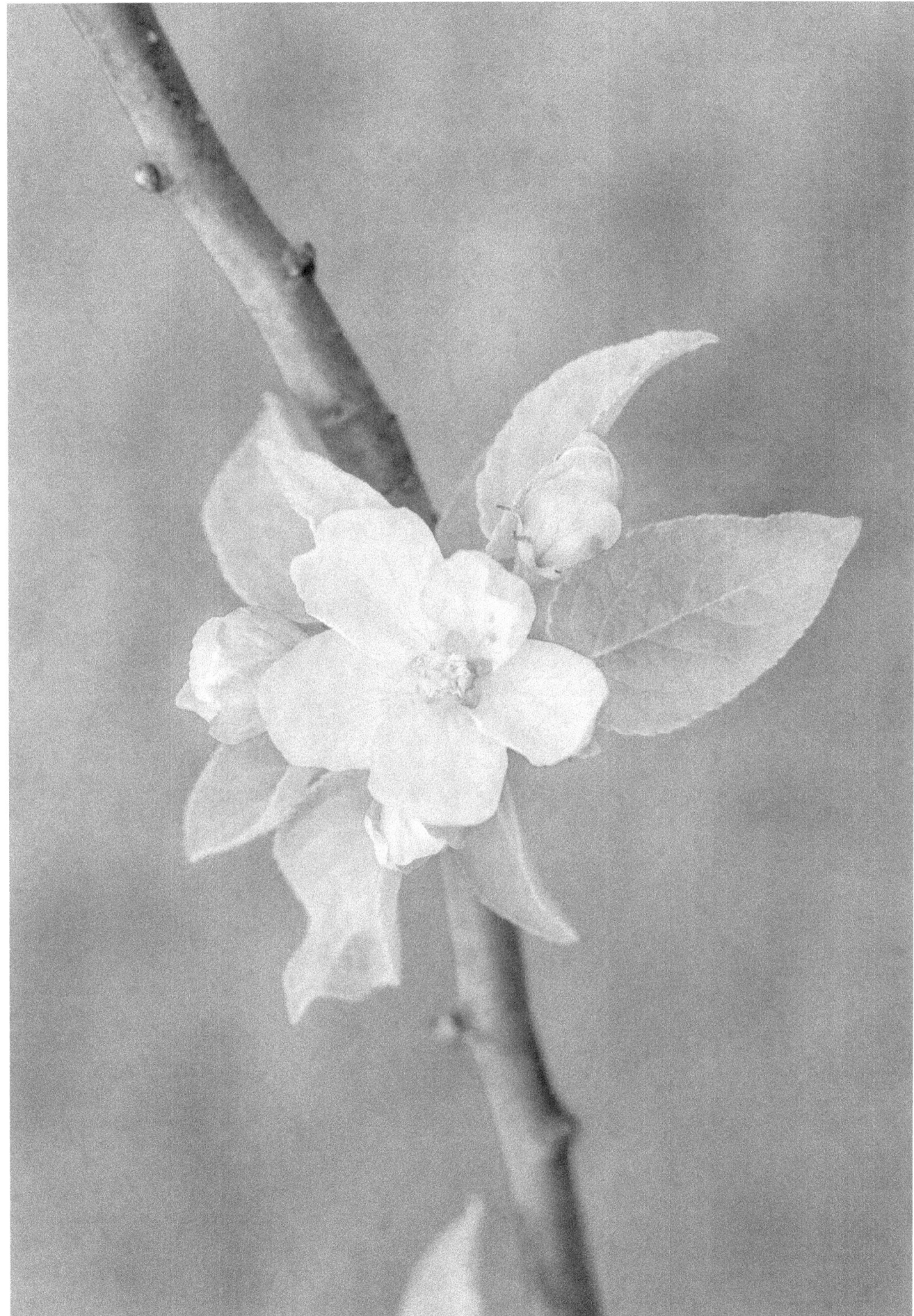

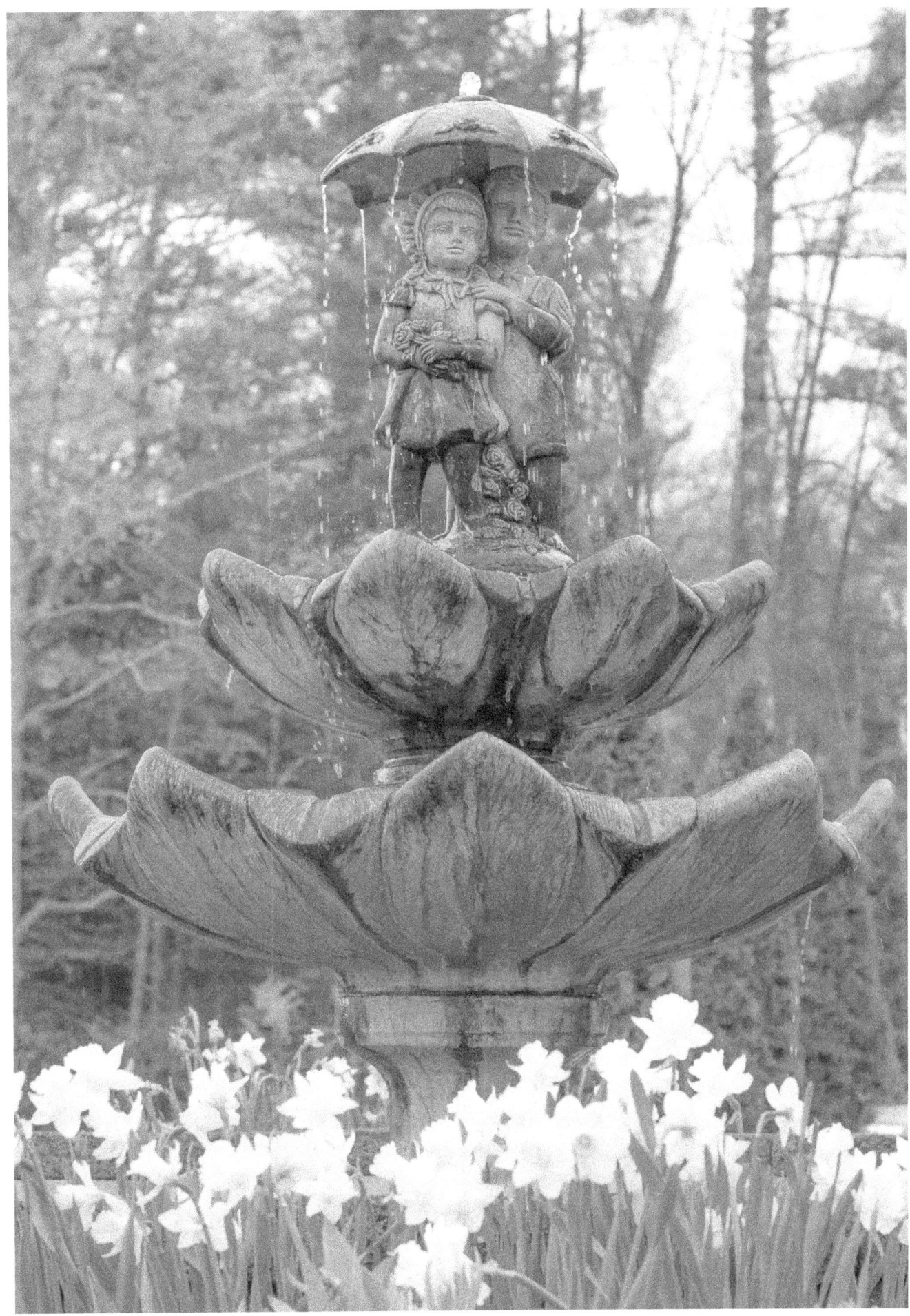

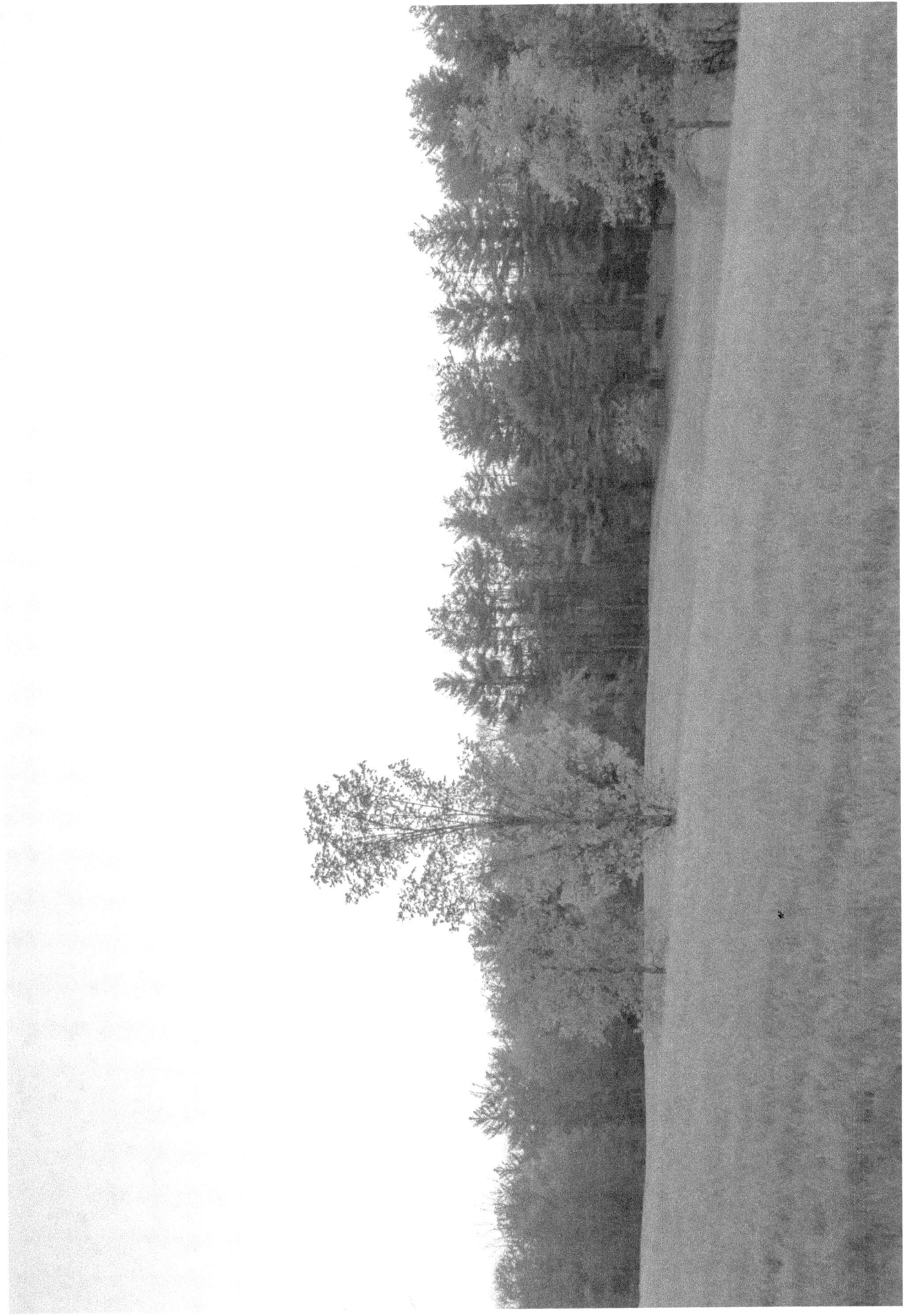

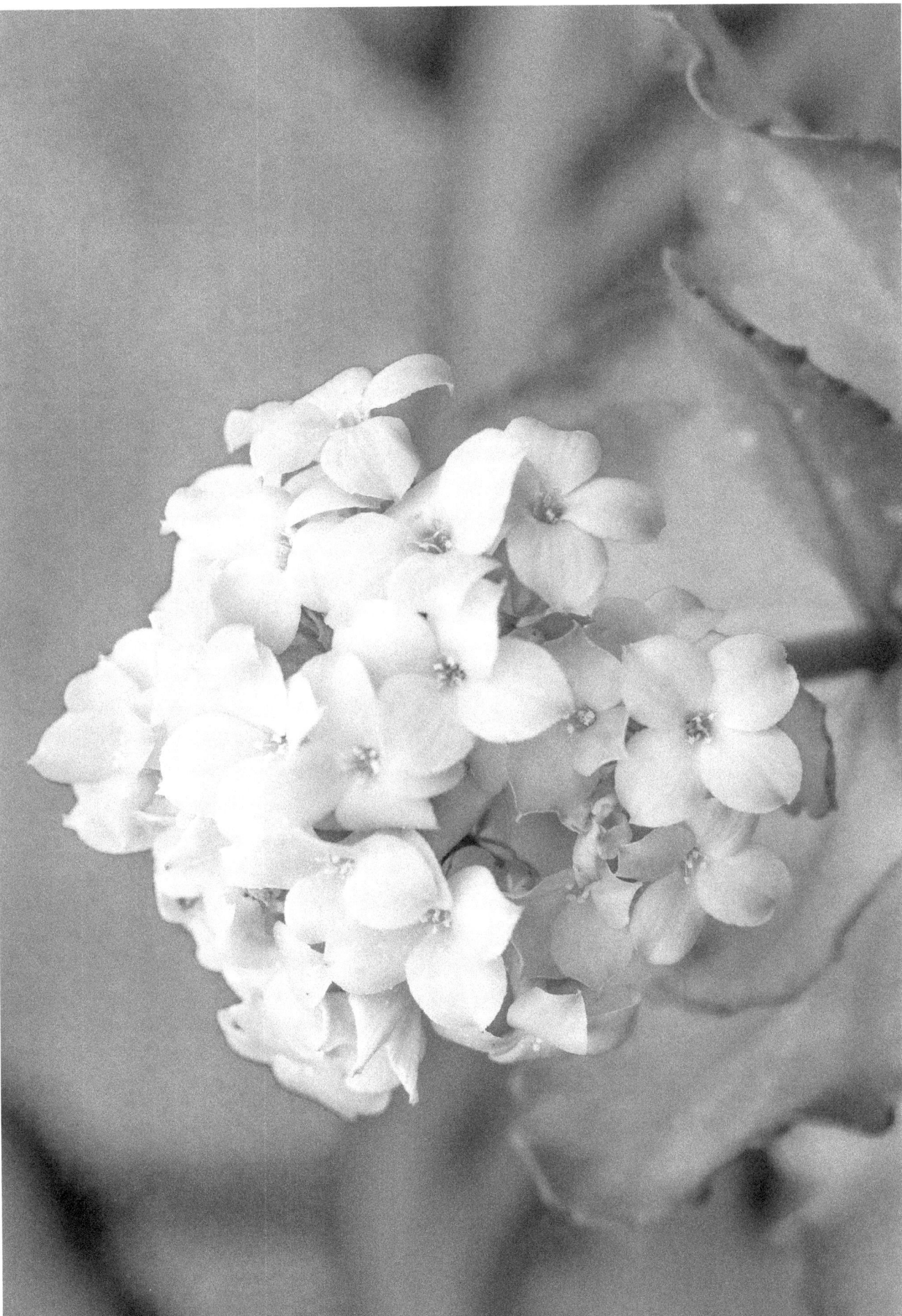

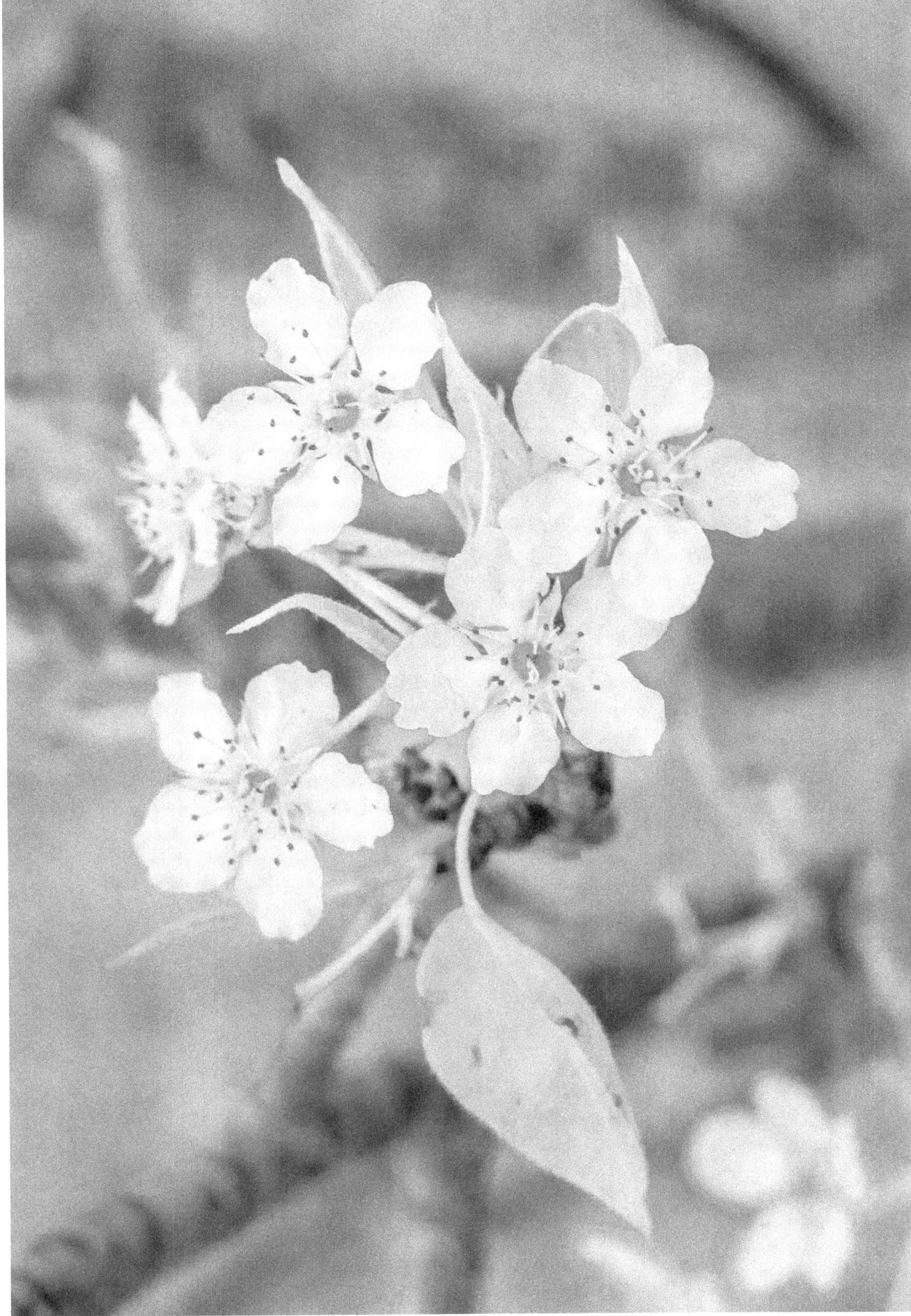

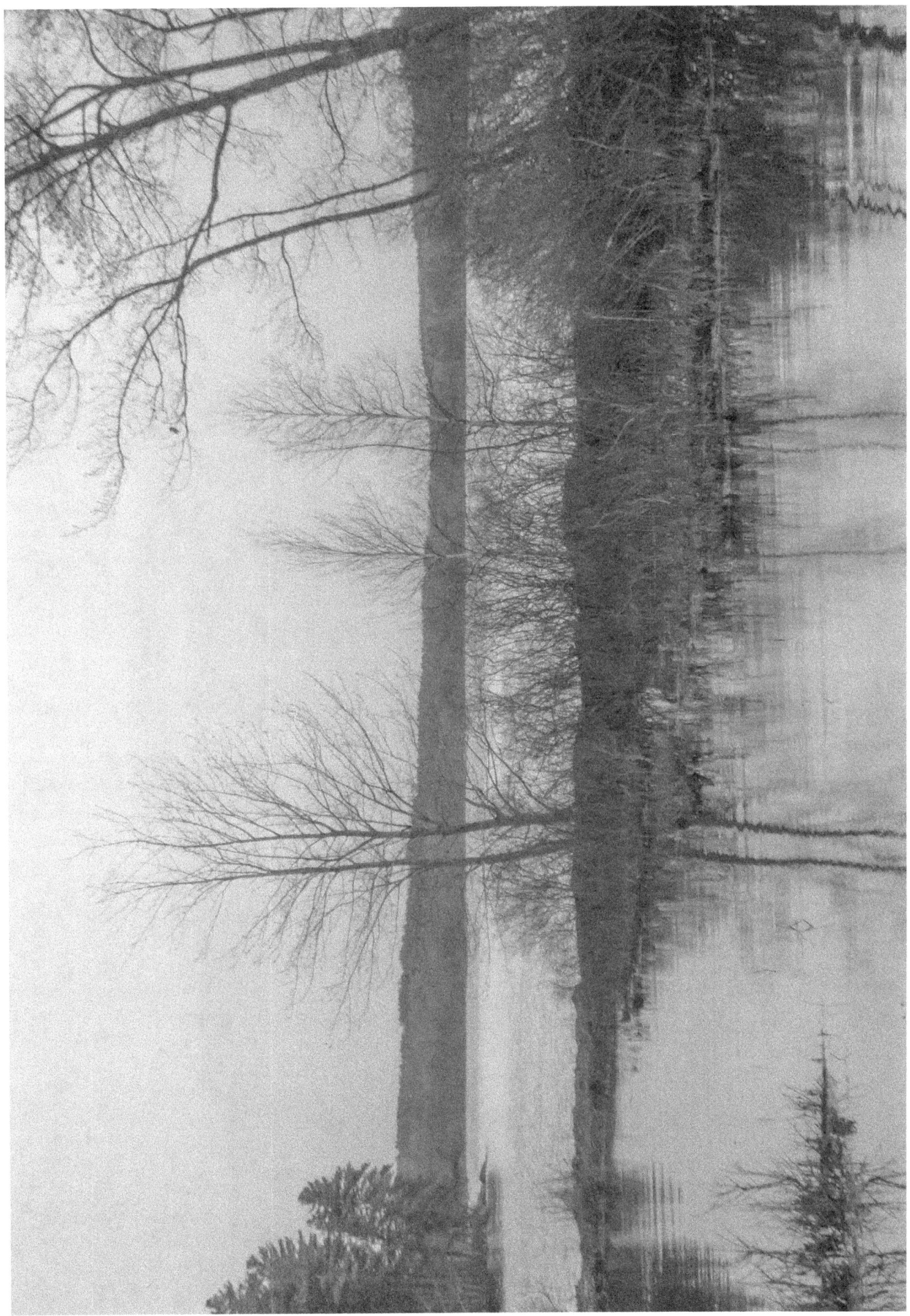

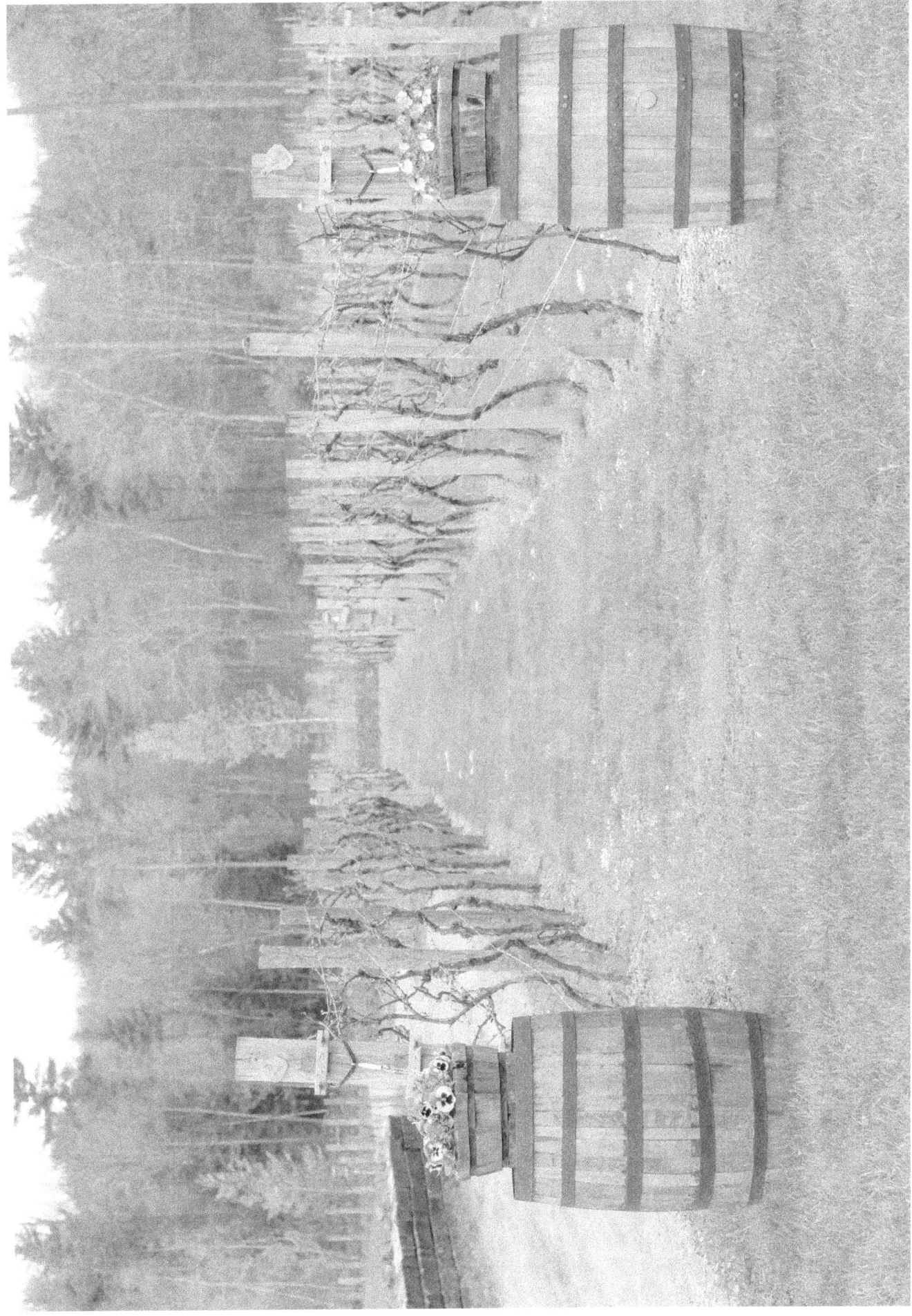

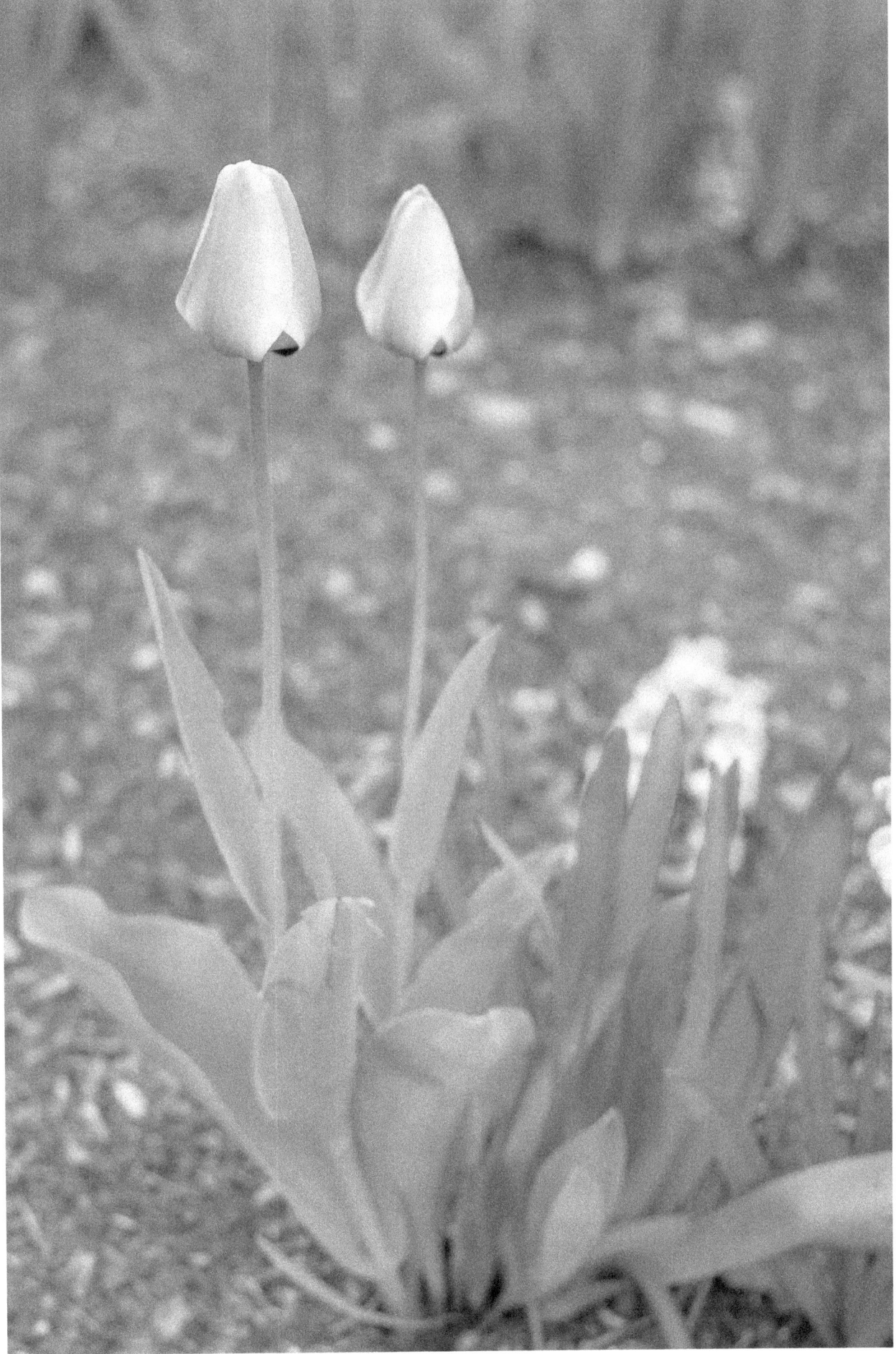

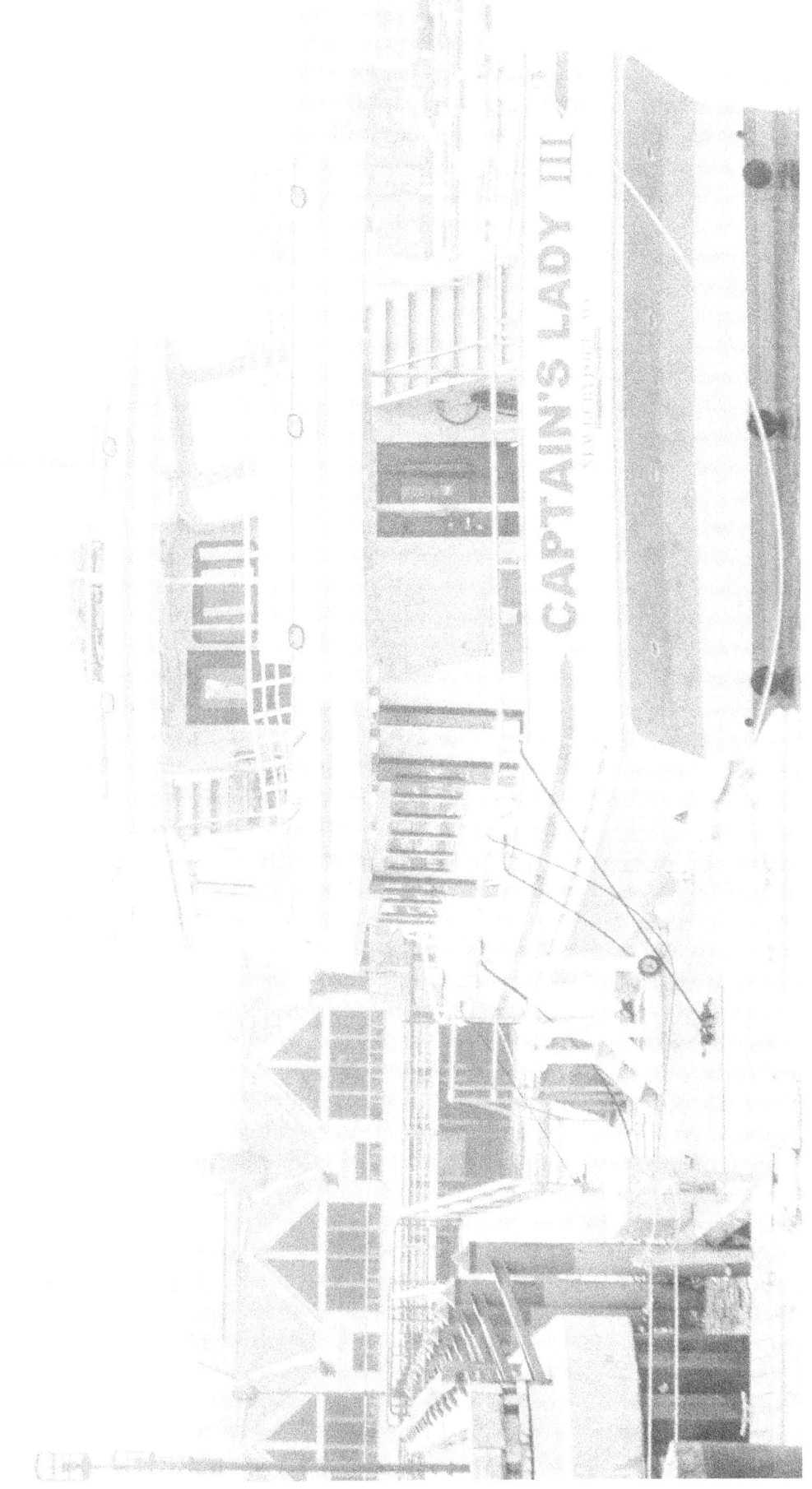

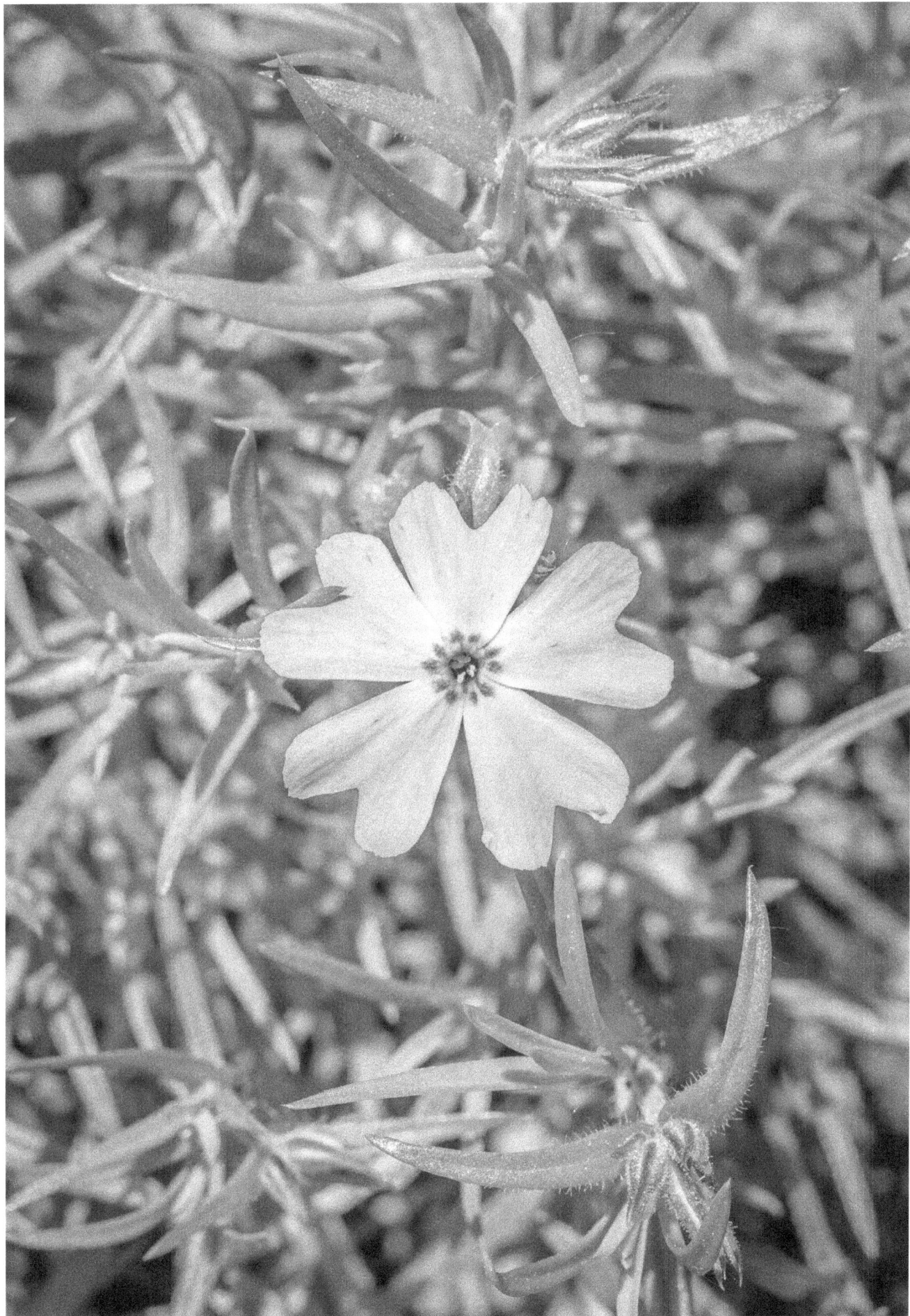

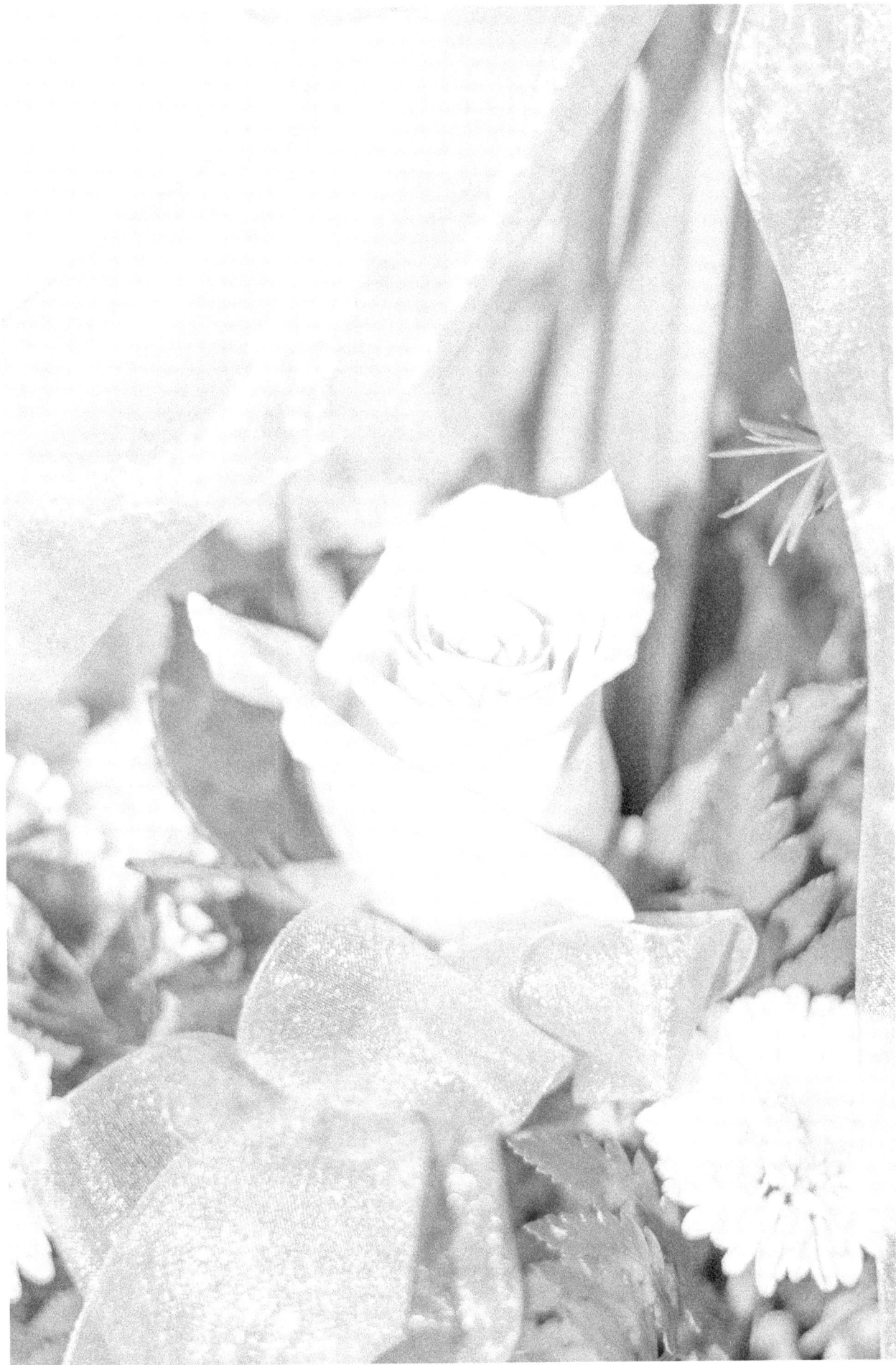

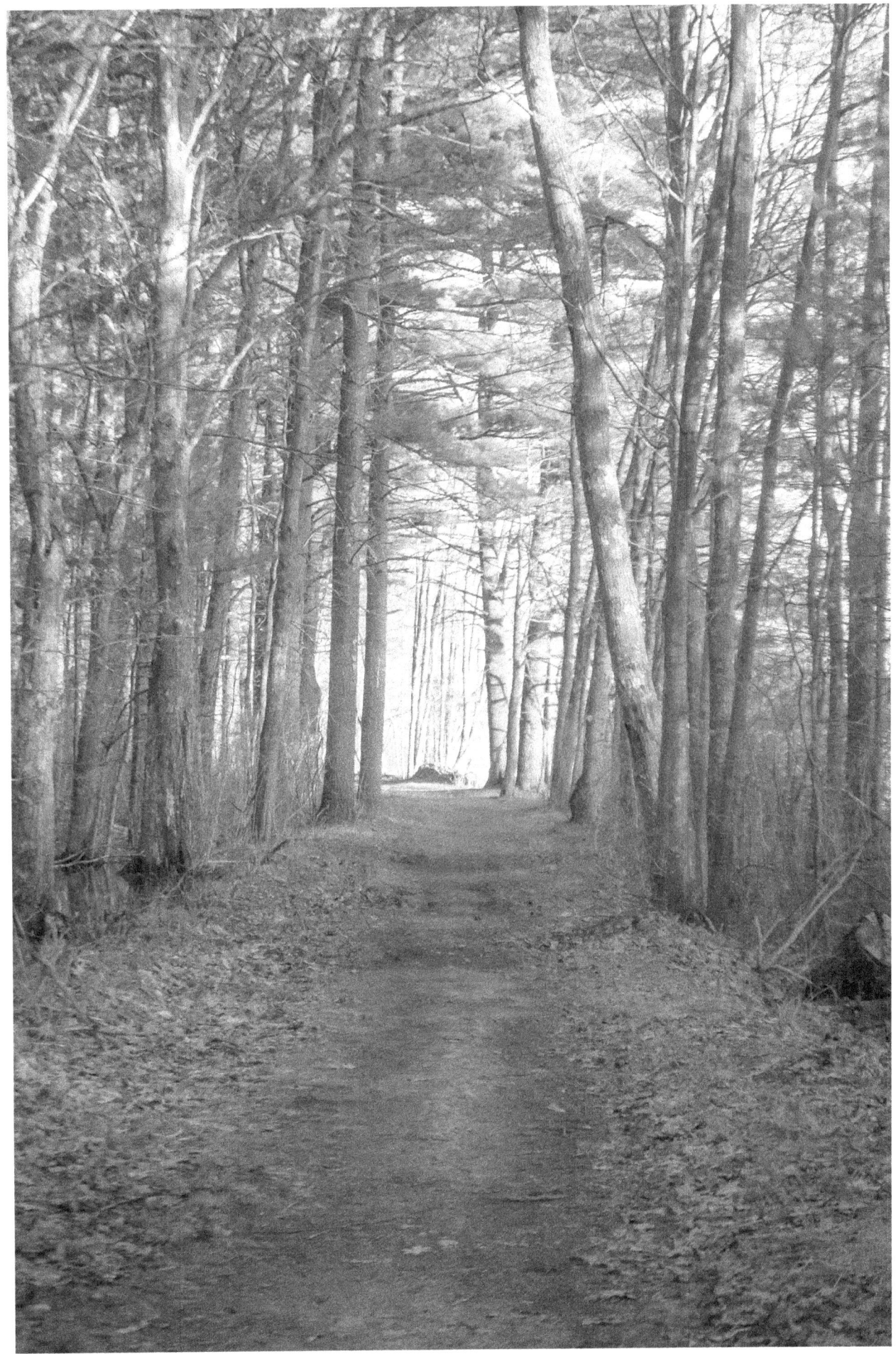

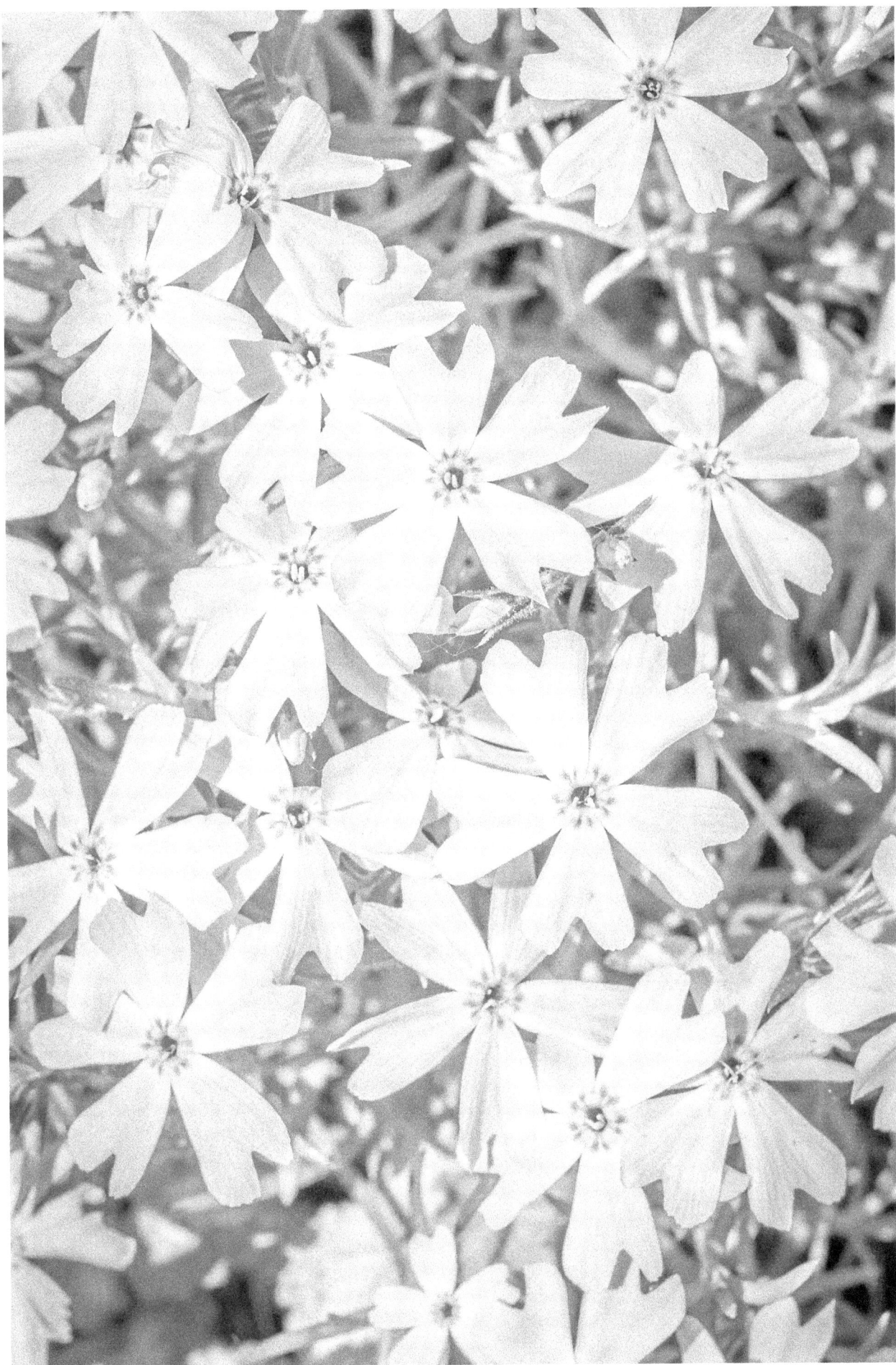

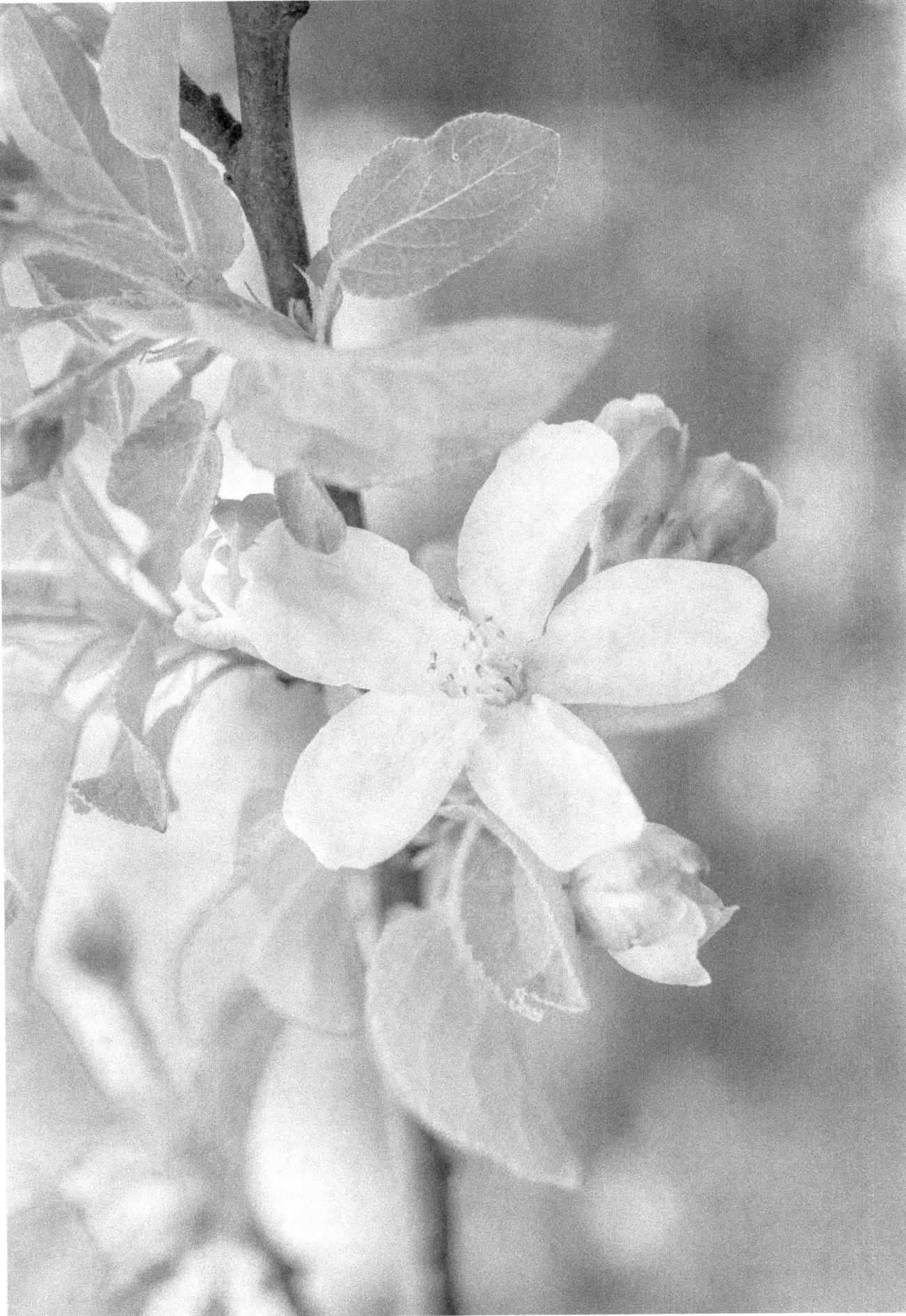

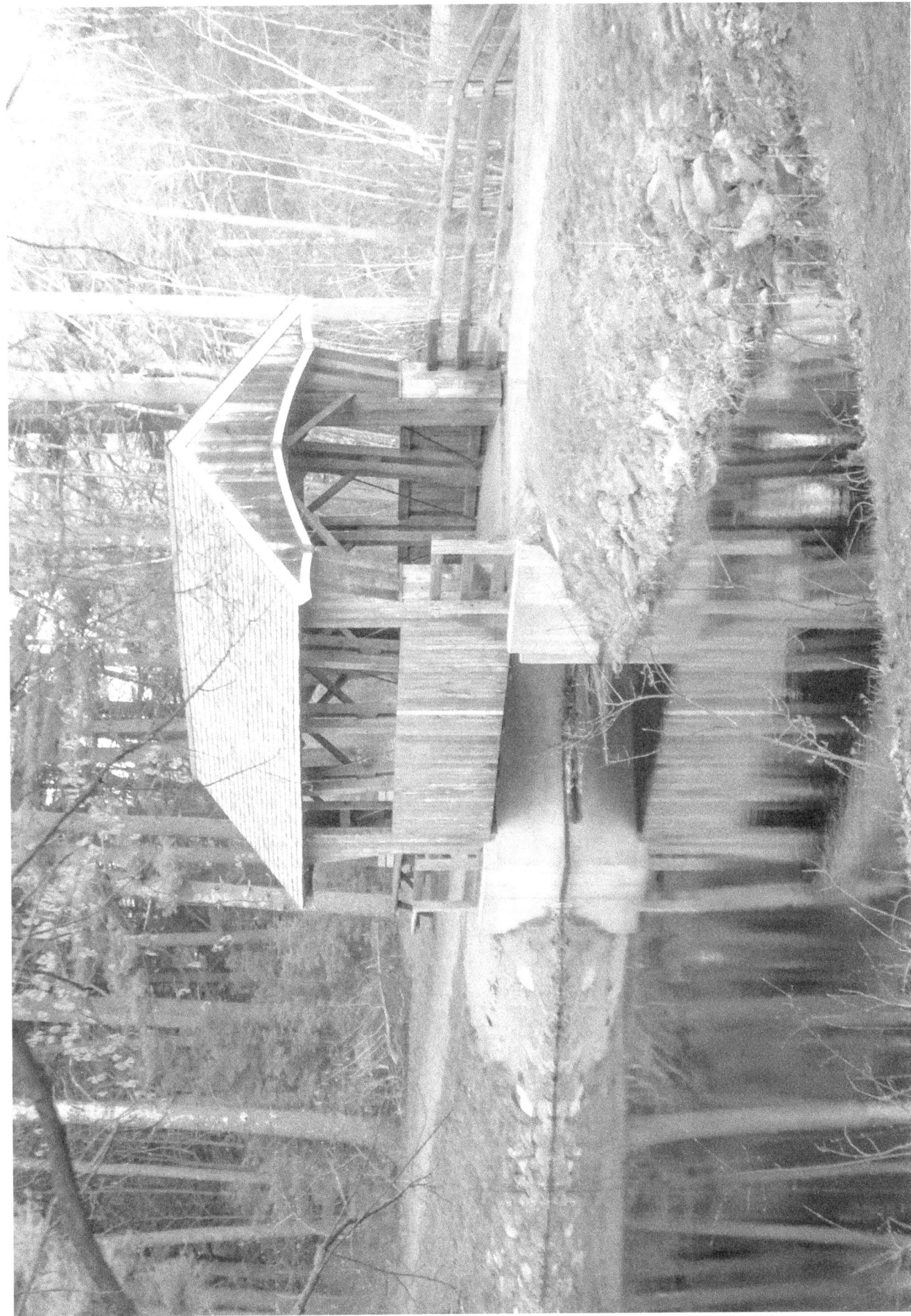

www.ingramcontent.com/pod-product-compliance
Lightning Source LLC
Chambersburg PA
CBHW081308180526
45170CB00007B/2618